MA

Many Questions

Reaching Out to those who have been in a place of Confusion With No Help!

Cover Design: Tamara Messiah Smith

In the United States of America

ISBN: 978-1499147643

BISAC: Religion/Christian Church/Growth

Dedication:

This book is dedicated to those who have not compromised the Gospel of Jesus Christ. To those who still testify to Gods Greatest his Majesty and Power; To the little town of Jonesboro, Georgia on Main street where the Father First Opened My eyes to SEE. I TRULY THANK God for you. To those who have been living in a lifestyle and has acknowledged in there heart that it's wrong and want out. To My Father that is in Heaven, thank you for my change coming. I give you Glory and take no Credit, for it all belongs to you. I truly thank God for all thirteen of my brothers and sisters who are far and near.

Christa Joy Martinez

ABOUT THE AUTHOR: (PREFACE)

WHY YOU SHOULD READ AND APPLY THIS
BOOK TO YOUR LIFE.......................

Contents...

INTRODUCTION...

Time Waits for No One: Trust and Believe in God!

CONTENTS

Preface (about the Author)

I Found Me! WHAT HAD BEEN LOCKED AWAY SO DEEP, WHAT HAD BEEN HID IN A PLACE THAT WAS MUCH TOO DARK TO VISIT. SO MANY CHAMBERS OF UNOPENED SECRETS, LIMITATIONS, Homosexuality, LIES, AND REGRET, Pain, and opened Wounds. ONE DAY WHILE LYING ON THE BED ASLEEP A HAND TOUCHED MY BACK AND IN A MILLISECOND: I FOUND ME. SO MANY MANY QUESTIONS, SO MANY MANY WEBS OF DARKNESS, that I truly didn't know how I'd gotten to such a place. MY SPIRIT LEAPED, I GAVE BIRTH TO THE REAL ME. JUDGE ME IF YOU WILL, GOD DID THIS FOR ME.

My life was never my own! From the age of three I can remember being in the bedroom and while my mother and friends were in the kitchen, I remember seeing the image of a DRAGON ON THE WALL. I NOW KNOW IT WAS THE IMAGE OF THE DEVIL. Out of 13 brothers and sisters in my family, I seemed to be the one always into something. Getting into trouble, are tearing things up (Or in my families voice "She always messes things up). I guess you could say that I never believed that things occurred for no Reason. I knew that there had to be something else that controlled life and this world. There were just too many circumstances, emotions, and chances in life that people were given to just be living. The Day I found JESUS CHRIST WAS THE DAY I FOUND THE PURPOSE OF MY LIVING. This book will help you to understand Why? Yes I no the first thing you are saying is I already know this answer but when I discovered How to Own My Authority Here on earth. THE LIGHTS CAME ON!!!! I pray that once you have read this book that the same light that came on for me will appear to you. Life can be a struggle when you have no direction.

Christa J. Martinez

Why Should You Read and Apply This Book?

PROVERBS 14:12

There is a Way which seemeth right unto man, but the end thereof or the ways of Death.

1 CORINTHIANS 10:13

THERE HATH NO TEMPTATION TAKEN HOLD OF YOU but such as is common to man. But God is faithful: He will not suffer you to be tempted beyond that which ye are able to bear, but with the temptation will also make a way to escape, that ye may be able to bear it.

Chapter 1

Life Will Always be a Challenge until you Truly Know Who You Are

---

The world today is constantly looking for answers to life. They continue to follow down the wrong paths from day to day because of the fears of this life. It continues to take many wrong turns, go down blind alleys, and into dead ends. Many have sought peace, vain and empty ways: mind-destroying drugs, homosexuality, Music, and other pointless purposes of life. The bible is the book that answers the basic questions of life. But it's up to you to let go of your fears and Receive Truth for Your Life. From the early age of three years old I began to recognize the questions that people ask in their late 40's. The Bible states that you are the crowning act of God's direct creation. Your body was formed in a way similar to the way artist forms a sculpture. God gave you body, a soul, and a spirit, each with its own needs and functions. When God created humans, He made them free. That is, God did not make them computers; He created them to be free to choose and to be. But at one point in our lives we all have chosen disobedience, resulting in the loss of fellowship with God. Therefore the ingredient missing in our lives is the presence of God and a True relationship with him. Some People feel as though this is not Real but they still experience a void in their life. This Void is truly why people feel the need to seek other things and to choose idols over what was created before Christ. It also explains why so many are restless, self seeking, and bored. Without God we are Lost.

The question of identity (who I am) is a question that people will ask until Christ Returns. You may have heard doctor's talk about something called an "identity crisis." The result of this search for identity is often a feeling of failure, lack of self-confidence, loneliness, Anger, Despair and so many other issues of life.

You are God's creation in search on a day to day basis of finding yourself. You must learn to confront your identity to find out your Purpose, God's plan and your Destiny that you will either walk into on earth are pursue until you die. The all time questions are all ways Who, What, When and How. Why am I here? You must come to the realization that because you are Gods Creation then you are HERE for a Purpose. God has a wonderful plan and purpose for your life. The first purpose on earth is to have relationship with God and to bring honor and glory to His name.

God loves you very much. He truly wants you to prosper and have good success. Your desires can become Reality once you learn how to tap into Your Authority that God has given every Believer that has sought to have a relationship with him. Truly God can and wants to bless your life and feel any and all Voids you may have.

Many ask, "Why was I given this life?" If you can only use this as a strategy to Move forward in your God given gifts and abilities that you were given. Ask yourself "What can I offer life?" The instant you comprehend that life is a gift of God and an opportunity for real service, you won't continue asking "Why?" These questions place great responsibility on you.

Most of the people Jesus called to be disciples were young. They were called to a life of total commitment, sacrifice and love to all those around them. Anyone who follows Christ must leave their past behind; who they once were, and Stop the things they used to do that wasn't pleasing to God. (Matt. 16:24). "He who is greatest among you shall be your servant" (Mat. 23:11). Only a few are willing to count the cost and pay the price (Luke 14:28). Christ's way is one of discipline. . You are instructed to "endure" hardship as a good soldier of Jesus Christ" (2 Tim. 2:3). As a follower of Christ, you can experience life in its fullness on earth, but God offers so much more. We cannot plan tomorrow's future. We cannot plan the changes that occur through the decades of generations even when we are faced with War, Illness and Death, Fear, and Disappointments in life. We must endure so that we can bring glory to our father which is in heaven. In the book of (John 14:1-6) the bible assures us of living eternal in our fathers house. So we understand that when we suffer in this lifetime we will reign in our father's house. So to answer the question comes up so often in this world today, " When is the World going to end", This is truly a question that we do not need to even concern ourselves with. When must learn to walk in the Will of God and Trust the Creators Path for Our lives. We do not know clearly what the future holds, but we know that God holds the future. It is and should be reassuring to know that the battle is not ours, it is truly the Lords. Being a Christian has been one of the most important priorities in my life. Once I found the Lord My main focus became getting to truly know him. I had to find a way to have a relationship with the father. Just as your natural father and you spend time together it is so urgent that you and God develop a relationship together. For me this was very challenging at the beginning because my biological father and Mother were absent in my life from the age of three. I truly had to step out on faith, So many of you will have to do the same. It will be like learning to ride a bicycle all over again. The only difference will be that now that your saved you will have full access to the fathers instructions. God has left a scriptural guideline that no one can fail which is the Holy Bible.

Jesus Himself extends the invitation to you in Revelation 3:20-"Behold, I stand at the door and knock. If anyone hears my voice and opens the door, I will come in to him and dine with him, and he with me." The door is the door of your heart, and the dining signifies fellowship and a relationship. Here is a sample prayer you can pray to receive Christ. But you can pray in your own words. Jesus is concerned more with your faith than with what you say with your mouth.

Chapter 2

What does it mean to be born again?

The term "born again" is taken from the words of Jesus in John 3:3, where He told Nicodemus the Pharisee that he must be born again. Just as you were puzzled the first time you heard that phrase, so was Nicodemus. Jesus lovingly took the time to explain to him the possibility of a spiritual life here on earth, different from the physical life, and which results in eternal life. Just as we are born into a physical family, we must be born again into a spiritual family, God's family of believers.

We learn from the Bible that "all have sinned and fall short of the glory of God" (Rom. 3:23). God is holy; man is a sinner. This is the reason a person must be born again. Sin separates us from God. God is holy, that is, without sin. Our sin, therefore, must be removed if we are ever to experience a communion with God in this life as well as eternally in heaven (Rom. 3:10-18, 23).

For this reason alone God sent His Son Jesus into the world. "For God did not send His Son into the world to condemn the world, but that the world through Him might be saved" John 3:17). If our own good works, religion, the church, or social standing could get us into heaven, then Christ would never have had to die (Eph. 2:8). Though our sins separate us from God, Christ bridges the gap by removing the sin. "For there is one God and one Mediator between God and men, the Christ Jesus" (1 Tim. 2:5).

Knowing all about Christ and His payment for sin, we can have full assurance that we can trust

God. When we accept his love for us and will for our lives we obtain new life. We must *receive* this gift of eternal life by an act of faith, an active belief in God's promise to remove our sins. "But as many as received Him, to them He gave the right to become children of God, even to those who believe in His name: who were born, not of blood, nor of the will of the flesh, nor of the will of man, but of God" (John 1:12, 13). To do this, first admit to God you are a sinner and be willing to turn from sin. Next, believe in your heart that God has raised Christ from the dead. Finally, invite Christ to come into your life and to control it. This is to receive Him as Savior and Lord (Rom. 10:13). If you are not saved the time is now. Don't let this opportunity Pass you by. Just Repeat these Words......

"Dear Lord, thank You for loving me. Thank You for dying on the cross for me. I know I am a sinner and cannot save myself. Please forgive all my sin. Jesus, right now, please come into my heart, save me, and changes me. I give my life to you, to follow you the rest of my life. Help me to live for you and to tell others what you have done for me this very moment. Thank You for answering my prayer and saving me. Amen?' You can be sure you are born again into the family of God because of His promise. "Most assuredly, I say to you, he who hears my word and believes in Him who sent me has everlasting life, and shall not come into judgment, but has passed from death into life" (John 5:24). "For whoever calls upon the name of the Lord shall be saved" (Rom. 10:13). And "the Spirit Himself bears witness with our spirit that we are children of God ..."(Rom. 8:16). Take the time now to share your decision with your parents, pastor, someone who can give you guidance that is saved to get you to the next step now that you are saved. Don't make the mistake and take your decision to someone who is unsaved because the blind cannot lead the blind.

Chapter 3

Temptation is Easy to give into when you

have No Direction?

WHEW! I WAS PRAISING GOD, SHOUTING, AND THANKING GOD THAT MY LIFE HAD BEEN CHANGED AT THE AGE OF 14 YEARS OF AGE. I began going to Church in one of my foster homes for a couple of months and learning that God truly loved me and that was how true love was supposed to really feel like. But one thing that I found out after coming home from that bible study when I gave my life to Christ was that growing up as an adolescent was not easy. Its definition is "preparing for maturity." Preparing indicates a time of learning and adjusting. Although no longer a child, you are not yet an adult. The teenage life is one that deals with in securities. So you will find yourself being exposed to things and before you have knowledge of it you are already involved. Every boy and girl must pass through this stage of life to become a grown man or woman. But for me I just seemed to have so many things against me. I was in a foster home with a total of six children and I thought everyone was always picking on me. I was being hit on, spit at, the refrigerator was locked and most of the times I found myself so hungry. I felt as though I was just being treated so badly. One day I just couldn't take it. The feeling of being a million dollars today but the next day worthless. I should have just been patient. The end result would have been wonderful earlier in my life but I didn't wait on God. Instead I ended up in a Homosexual relationship for eleven years of my life. I Had SEEN IT ALL. I Had DONE IT ALL. I Had WITNESSED IT ALL. I USED TO TALK TO PEOPLE AND TELL THEM THAT IT WAS OK TO LIVE THAT LIFESTYLE, DON'T BE FOOLED, I USED TO SAY THAT ONE SIN WAS NO GREATER ARE LESS THAN ANOTHER. DON'T BE FOOLED. THAT SOME OF THE BOOKS WERE MISSING IN THE BIBLE AND THAT WAS WHY PEOPLE MADE BEING GAY SOUND SO BAD .PLEASE DON'T BE FOOLED. I was too young I had gotten too deep in. I was speaking of things that I was told and not how I truly felt are what I'd truly experienced. The fact of the matter is I would go home at night thinking about the life that I could have had. Was walking a life of denial and knew the truth. I was going through verbal abuse on a day to day basis. I was sharing my body with others because I felt as though I had to. I had accepted rape in my life because I thought it was part of the territory. Yes, Rape. I had been molested in a foster home during my early teenage years and began to develop so much hate for men without me even realizing it. But then living a homosexual life style I'd accepted the fact that although I didn't want to have sex with women it was the "Thing" so I went along with it. I became a Piece of Meat, Just something for someone to have and slowly lost all value for myself and my true identity. As a teenager you will have a great need to talk and share these confusing changes and times in your life but I didn't. For me it was Homosexuality but for you it could be something else. I ran away to a friend's house. I had completely given up. I began living the way that made me feel good. I would sit and think that I could take care of myself. So that is what I did. By the time, I'd turned the age of sixteen (16) I was in a homosexual lifestyle that I thought I fit in. My lover at the time was twenty-eight (28) years old and I thought she knew everything. Yes, I was only sixteen years old and I fell pray to the cares of this world. I thought she had so much to offer me. I found myself taking nude pictures, lingerie modeling, and going to clubs before I could even purchase a drink. I never felt anything but I moved on what I could see. My feeling and Emotions got the best of me. I moved on the fact that my well being was going to be taking care of. This was so important for me at that age. Finally I felt as though someone understood me and I wasn't alone.

There I thought I'd found the answers to all of my life problems so I would do what ever it took to stay secure, not hungry, and loved. I thought like many you today that I had to " HAVE MONEY". You will find there are those who care about your needs and those that just want you to give them a reason to exist. Low self esteem, inadequacies, feeling that you don't fit in because of you look, dress are mindset were the majority of the reasons that those who had gotten into the "Life Style" talked about. If you don't have the right direction then you will be tempted in more than one way and you will easy fall prey to the predators that are out there. People who are hurt and have been hurt developed a false since of Who they are and become lost to the fact that they can't decipher the right from the wrong decision. People often say talk to your parents, and consult your pastor or youth workers but

28

the end result was that I didn't have any of that. The only thing I had was me. I was put into foster care at the age of three and had been in and out of shelters, orphans and foster homes. How do you know who to trust and who you can believe and count on when your entire life has been so unstable. Every one seemed as though they were just concerned about themselves. Too busy to stop and discern the fact that your life is headed in the wrong direction. What truly happened to those older grandmothers, and mothers who would see a child going wrong and would have the boldness to day "Stop baby you are headed down the wrong way. As I passed through these teen years and being a early adult no one talked about God. No one talked about Love, Heaven or Hell. It was like The Gay Society was in a world of its own. My beliefs were tried, questioned and then they became obsolete. It had me!

29

Everything that I'd ever learned morals, values, life skill, and discernment didn't exit anymore. I was just considered a Snack, A Piece, and the sad part was I knew that Hell was where I was going to lift my eyes. Please take heed to my life story don't give into temptation if you can avoid it. The scriptures states in *1 Peter 5:8* Be sober, be vigilant; because your adversary the devil, as a roaring lion, walketh about, seeking whom he may devour:

For this reason it is imperative that you establish a firm foundation of Christian principles and morals. Believing and acting on these is important. But do not make the mistake of not knowing *why* you believe and act. Take the time to learn the Scriptures. When confusion confronts you, you can defeat it with the truth, that is, through Jesus Christ and His Word. "You shall know the

truth, and the truth shall make you free"
(John 8:32).

Chapter 4

CAN I BE A HOMOSEXUAL AND STILL GO TO HEAVEN?

Too many Times I hear People say that life is about chances! For a very long time I believed that I could still go to heaven and be a Homosexual. At least this is what the GAY CHURCHES and communities try to teach you. I Can truly say the answer is No, AND FOR THOSE WHO ARE LOOKING FOR A SCIENTIST TO AGREE WITH YOU....THERE HAS NOT BEEN ONE! It is an Abomination to God! IT'S TIME FOR YOU TO HEAR THE WHOLE TRUTH. At best, the evidence for a genetic and/or biological basis to homosexual orientation is inconclusive. In fact, "In fact AND I QUOTE, since the early 1990s, numerous studies attempting to establish a genetic cause for homosexuality have not proven to be valid or repeatable – two important requirements for study results to become accepted as fact in the scientific community. Because of this, the current thinking in the scientific community is that homosexuality is likely caused by a complex interaction of psychosocial, environmental and possible biological factors. And the two leading national psychiatric and psychological professional groups agree that, so far, there are no conclusive studies supporting any specific biological or genetic *cause* for homosexuality. In sum, there is no scientific or DNA test to tell us if a person is homosexual, bisexual or even heterosexual for that matter. And since nobody is "born gay," it's clear that sexual orientation is, at its core, a matter of *how one defines oneself* – not a matter of biology or genes".(True NEWS.ORG") So the bottom line is that people do what feels good, look good, taste and what they feel. We all know that at some point in time our emotions and feeling have fooled us and we have erred. So we must define the word feeling, "

The definition of a Feeling is

A sensation experienced through touch. **A** physical sensation. A feeling of warmth.

Having **the** ability to react or feel emotionally; sentient; sensitive.

Easily moved emotionally; sympathetic. A feeling heart.

Expressive **of** sensibility or emotion, a feeling glance

The Definition of an Emotion

A mental state that arises spontaneously rather than through conscious effort and **is** often accompanied by physiological changes; **a** feeling.

The emotions of joy, sorrow, reverence, hate, and love.

A state **of** mental agitation or disturbance.

Spoke unsteadily in a voice that betrayed his emotion.

The part of the consciousness that involves feeling; sensibility.

So the Bottom line is NO YOU CANNOT GO TO HEAVEN AS A HOMOSEXUAL!!! You may read more in depth scriptures in the book of Leviticus 18 and 20.

We must recognize that Holiness is still Holiness. The bible declares that we are to be holy as he is holy. So in following the life of Christ we can't allow ourselves to worship idols are create others laws to live by to please our emotions or feelings.

Chapter 5

What is Holiness?

Holiness is to be a vital part of every believer's life, rather than of the lives of the exceptional few. In fact, an entire book of the Bible, the book of Leviticus, is devoted to the subject of holiness. The word "holy" is found in different forms six hundred times throughout the Bible.

Holiness is defined as being morally blameless. It is to be separated from sin and therefore consecrated to God. The word signifies "separation to God" and the conduct befitting those so separated. This seems like an impossible goal. How can God command us, "You shall be holy; for I am holy" (Lev. 11:44; 1Pet. 1:16)? God's holiness is perfect freedom from all evil. Let us grasp the true meaning of the statement. Just as we are told to "be holy:' we are also admonished to "pursue....holiness" (Heb.12:14), that is, to seriously strive for it. We have the life of Christ for an example. "Therefore be followers of God as dear children" (Eph. 5:1) literally means "keep on becoming imitators of God?' To be holy is to turn from sin and self and seek conformity to the nature of God. We cannot undertake such a work in our own strength and power. Faith in Christ, accompanied by the strength of the Word of God, will give us the necessary stamina to walk in obedience to God's will. He has not left us in our own weakness. We have the promises that God works in us (Phil. 2:13), that the Holy Spirit guides us (John 16:13), and that Christ's power suffices for us (Eph. 3:20). Christ died and rose again to share His very own life and nature with us. He died, not only to forgive us, but to make us like Himself. Christ has redeemed us in order that "we should be holy and without blame before Him in love" (Eph. 1:4).

By God's grace we are enabled to adopt a lifestyle of holiness, that is, obedience to the will of God. With His help, by guarding our minds and emotions, controlling our appetites and desires, we develop holy habits that will remain with us as we grow. These vital teachings are so important because it will prevent us from just sinning habitually.

CHAPTER 6

What is Sin?

It is important to understand that secular society has tried to eliminate the word "sin" from our vocabulary. Despite the effort, all one has to do is read the papers, listen to the news broadcasts, or look into his own heart to realize that we all have been stained with sin. Dr. Karl Menninger, of the Menninger Psychiatric Institute, now warns that denying "sin" as a fact of our culture is a serious mistake. See his book *whatever Became of Sin?* The Bible tells us that the word "sin" literally means "to miss the mark' It is the picture of an expert marksman aiming with all his concentration but failing to hit his target. The Bible states: "Whoever commits sin also commits lawlessness, and sin is lawlessness" (1 John 3:4). "All unrighteousness is sin," (1 John 5:17). "For whatever is not from faith is sin" (Rom. 14:23). "Therefore, to him who knows to do good and does not do it, to him it is sin" (James 4:17). Anything that violates the Ten Commandments, the Golden Rule (Matt. 7-12), the Sermon on the Mount, or any other command of God, except the *ceremonial* laws of the Old Testament, is missing the standard that God has established. The ceremonial laws of the Old Testament worship, including sacrifices and purification, no longer apply to us, because Christ fulfilled all of the laws for us. No wonder the Bible teaches, "For all have sinned and fall short of the glory of God" (Rom. 3:23).

Every person should know that God clearly warns, "...be sure your sin will find you out" (Num. 32:23). This is a warning to Christians as well as non-Christians. My sin will find me out, and your sin will find you out. Let's analyze the subject of sin, using the Scriptures.

First, every young person should realize that there is pleasure in sin. "By faith Moses, when he became of age, refused to be called the son of Pharaoh's daughter, choosing rather to suffer affliction with the people of God than to enjoy the passing pleasures of sin" (Heb. 11:24, 25). Never suppose there is no pleasure in sin. Sin is easy, and it is often an attempt to escape from reality by such means as drugs, drinking, and difficult sexual behavior. Satan has made these very enjoyable-but only for a time.

Second, the pitfalls of sin. "...and that they may come to their senses and escape the snare of the devil, having been taken captive by him to do his will" (2 Tim. 2:26). When you least expect it, the devil will Pull the rug from beneath you. He has set a trap for every young person.

Third, the progression of sin. "Let no one say when he is tempted, 'I am tempted by God'; for

God cannot be tempted by evil, nor does He Himself tempt anyone. But each one is tempted when he is drawn away by his own desires and enticed. Then, when desire has conceived, it gives birth to sin; and sin when it is full grown, brings forth death" (James 1:13-15). Every "kick" has a kickback Sin fascinates, then assassinates; thrills, then kills; enjoys, then destroys. Write this quote in the front of your Bible:

"Sin will take you farther than you want to go, keep you longer than you want to stay, and cost you more than you want to." Sin is like leprosy or cancer: it begins with small blemishes or small groups of abnormal cells, then begins to destroy the body. God regards sin somewhat like a disease. It is abnormal, destructive, disturbs bodily functions, weakens, causes pain, deadens the senses, blinds, and cripples.

Sin is contagious and powerful. Even death doesn't cure sin. He that dies filthy will be filthy fur eternity. The Fourth penalty of sin. "The wages of sin is death..." (Rom. 6:23). Sin is no respecter of persons. You can come from a good family and be active in church. You may be led to follow the example of the crowd, intending to sin "only once?' But "do not be deceived, God is not mocked;

For whatever man sows that will he also reap. For he who sows to his flesh will of the flesh reap corruption, but he who sows to the Spirit will of the Spirit reap everlasting life" (Gal. 6:7, 8). Your sin will find you in your face, in your conscience, someday in your children, and then in judgment. But God has an alternative. Read the rest of Romans 6:23-"but the gift of God is eternal life in Christ Jesus our Lord?' The Fifth pardon of sin is accepting that Jesus Christ came to this earth almost two thousand years ago, lived a perfect life, and laid down His life in your place. He paid for your sins. Remember, "...without shedding of blood there is no remission" of sin (Heb. 9:22). Receive

His free gift today. By His wounds we are healed. There is evidence of having been healed if you demonstrate the following characteristics: Confess Christ as Savior; Worship God the Father, Son, and Holy Spirit; and live a moral life.

Chapter 7

Why do I continue to Fail?

There is a very simple reason why you and I continue to fail: "For all have sinned and fall short of the glory of God" (Rom. 3:23). Though we bear the image of God (Gen. 1:26, 27) there operates within us a bent toward sin. Even the great apostle Paul had this struggle: "I find then a law, that evil is present with me, the one who wills to do good" (Rom. 7:21). Having this law of sin in our lives, shall we give in to discouragement? Certainly not! This is exactly what Satan would like to see us do: quit, give up hope. But we need not even think this way, for we have the sure promise of God: "You are of God, little children, and have overcome them, because He who is in you is greater than he who is in the world" (1 John 4:4). Any circumstance, no matter how bad it may seem, is being allowed in your life by God. Therefore it is going to work together for your good, if you will only trust God and give it time (Rom. 8:28).

The Bible tells us, "The heart is deceitful above all things, and desperately wicked; who can know it?" (Jer. 17:9). There are times when we are not honest about our actions. Rather than face the guilt or consequences, we justify our actions, passing them off as small mistakes. Many times we simply convince ourselves that we did not sin, even though the Bible condemns our actions clearly. This will bring our downfall and will only lead farther away from God. Even though we may admit sin in our lives, we may not take the time to seek true forgiveness by repenting, or *turning away*, from that sin. Unconfessed sin drives a wedge between you and God.

Perhaps you are overconfident about your Christian walk, feeling that you would never sin as so many others do. Beware! Temptation attacks each of us in a personal way, at the weakest point. Paul warned

us, "Therefore let him who thinks he stands take heed lest he fall" (1Cor. 10:12). Do not tempt yourself by needless exposure to evil. Be careful about the places you go, the friends you select, the shows you watch, what you do with your time and priorities.

Certainly we should never feel, because Christ has already paid for our sins, that we have a license to sin. Romans 6:1, 2 proclaim, "What shall we say then? Shall we continue in sin that grace may abound? Certainly not! How shall we who died to sin live any longer in it?" Presumptuousness or complacency in sin is a very dangerous attitude and one that requires counsel and correction.

If you are going to endure the spiritual war, you will need to believe God's Word in faith. When you doubt, you have no foundation on which to stand, you have no armor with which to fight. It will then be easy to fall and be captured by your enemy, the devil, Read the story of the temptation of Jesus by Satan in the wilderness. Each time, Jesus overcame the temptation with the Word of God. Follow His example by memorizing Scripture to help you in the daily battle, what is God doing in your life right now? Do you have a regular quiet time in which God can speak to you in His Word? A daily time alone with God is an absolute necessity if you are ever to achieve the discipline and perseverance you need as a Christian. A certain man trained two dogs for public performances. But one dog or the other always responded more quickly to commands than the other. "It's simple:' he said, "Whichever dog I want to perform better is the one I give special attention to during the week, I feed him well, play with him often, and show him a lot of affection. He becomes strong and willing to obey me. Naturally, the dog I spend more time with is always a better performer."Does this sound like your life in Christ? Do you feed your faith, spend time with God and with other Christians, have a willingness to serve Him? Or are you content just to "get by" and ignore Him most of the time? If so, you will never win your battles.

The Christian life is a growing and learning experience. You cannot expect overnight perfection. Rather, through a lifelong process of training, you learn to persevere and overcome your sin and weaknesses. Failure ought to be a stepping-stone to success. "We also glory in tribulations, knowing that tribulation produces perseverance; and perseverance, character, and character, hope. Now hope does not disappoint, because the love of God has been poured out in our hearts by the Holy Spirit who was given to us" (Rom. 5:3-5).

God knows we cannot be perfect-"For a righteous man may fall seven times and rise again" (Prov.24:16). But He does give us grace to please Him: "let us lay aside every weight, and the sin which so easily ensnares us, and let us run with endurance the race that is set before us, looking to Jesus, the author and finisher of our faith..." (Heb. 12:1, 2).

Chapter 8

What is Prayer?

Prayer is communication with God. Just as you talk daily with your earthly friends because you care about them and enjoy being with them, to let your needs be known, to thank them for all they do, so you should also communicate with God daily. Even though God knows your heart and your future, you cannot ignore Him, or your relationship with Him will diminish. If you love Him, you will desire communication with Him. "I will bless the Lord at all times: His praise shall continually be in my mouth"(Ps. 34:1).

Following the perfect example of Christ, we learn that prayer is necessary for all of us if we are to have the power to do God's will. In Matthew

26:39 we read of Christ's prayer as He spoke of His reluctance to face the pain of the cross; but desiring above all to do His Father's will, He sought the power in prayer to do so. Christ also taught us prayer as the key to receiving. "Ask, and it will be given to you; seek, and you will find; knock, and it will be opened to you" (Matt. 7:7). Prayer also gives us an opportunity to express our gratitude for all that God has done in our lives. Jesus Himself prayed, "Father, I thank You that You have heard Me" (John 11:41). The Scriptures give several ingredients for a successful prayer life. In Matthew 6:6 Jesus teaches us to pray in private. Prayer groups are important and there is power in unity, but without a quiet time alone with God we will have no spiritual power. The prayer of the Christian must be *persistent* (Luke 11:8), *bold* (Heb. 4:16), *in faith* (Mark 11:24), *specific* (Luke 11:11), and *in Jesus' name* (John 16:23, 24). Even with all of the above practices in prayer, there will be prayers which do not seem to be answered. Again, God's Word gives the knowledge to understand. Your request may not be granted because:

- It is not God's will for your life (1John 5:14, 15).
- It is not God's timing (Ps. 37:7).
- It is for the wrong motive (James 4:3).

- Unconfessed sin is blocking the way (Ps. 66:8; James 5:16).

- Strife exists between *you* and another *(Matt. 5:23, 24).*

- Family division is evident (1 Pet. 3:7).

Now let us try to put prayer into a simple form for your daily use, The acrostic ACTS is a guideline you can use without confusion: God is worthy of our praise and we should begin each day with adoration of His Greatness, love, forgiveness, faithfulness, and holiness. God has many attributes worthy of praise. Psalm 138) His death on the cross, we still must ask His forgiveness in order to keep our relationship growing in love. Confession is more than saying "I admit it; I'm sorry?' and to ask God to help you feel as much hatred for sin as He Himself does. Then and only then can you forsake the sin that holds you. Try Psalm 51. We should walk every day of our lives with a heart of thanksgiving. This is the part of your prayer time in which you can thank God for all He has given you, for the answers to prayer you have received, for the many blessings, and for all you are learning. A grateful heart is one that is blessed abundantly again and again. Try Psalm 103. Supplication is the act of requesting. There are many types of requests. Pray for and claim by name the salvation of those you are concerned about. Now that you know how to pray, you may say, "But when? I really don't have the time." You must make time. Our conversation flows so easily on the telephone, at a party, at a friend's home; yet somehow we are afraid to talk to God. Prayer is our privilege, given to us by the death of Christ on the cross. Establish a time of the day for prayer, preferably before you start the day, while your thoughts are clear and free from distraction.

Chapter 9

What is the Best Way to Study the Bible?

Many good intentions have gone astray because of lack of good planning. This is especially true in Bible study. The idea of opening the Bible anywhere and reading, or jumping from book to book and chapter to chapter, has its occasional advantage; but there is no substitute for systematic Bible study.

Why study the Bible anyway? First and foremost, because we are commanded: "Be diligent [study] to present yourself approved to God, a worker who does not need to be ashamed, rightly dividing the word of truth" (2 Tim. 2:15). Next, because it is God's Word to us, as well as our guidebook (2 Tim. 3:16). We need to be able to understand the Bible so that we can share its good news with others. By learning to correctly interpret the Bible, we will not be deceived by false doctrine. The Word of God is alive and powerful and can direct our hearts (Heb. 4:12). It gives us strength to overcome sin (Eph. 6:17; Ps, 119:11). It offers hope and direction during times of struggle (Rom. 15:4). As a result of study and obedience of the Word of God, we will achieve God's goals for our lives, according to God's promise (Josh. 1:8).

There are many ways to study the Word of God, but without consistency none of them will suffice: Hear the Word taught, read the Scriptures, memorize verses. Any time you learn the Word of God, take the time to *apply* the passages: How do these words affect my world, my church, or my Christian life in general and in particular? As a result of reading these passages, what action must I take to comply with what they say?

Perhaps you have tried to read the Bible before without success. God's Word is set apart for the spiritual man (1 Cor. 2:14). The riches and treasures of its pages are hidden to the one who has never been born again or to the one who harbors sin in his heart.

Begin each special study time with prayer for understanding, asking God to reveal areas of your life He seeks to develop or correct through His Word. Make it a personal time and a practical time for aid in daily living. By memorizing key verses, the application and learning will continue throughout your life. Also allow the Word to become grounded in your heart by sharing with others what you have learned. Good news is always better when shared with others.

Chapter 10

How Can I know Gods Will for My Life?

Perhaps it should be pointed out that all people do not find God's will concerning full- time Christian service in the same way. While there is no magic formula, there are biblical principles that should be helpful:

1) God loves you and has a plan for your life. Never forget this truth. He has a unique plan for each day as well as for your Future, You may not know in advance all that this plan involves, but God will unfold it as you obey and wait on Him.

2) God will go out of His way to show you His will. He wants you to do His will more than you

want to do it and so will provide clear guidance. "I will instruct you and teach you in the way you should go" (Ps.32:8).

3) God has given you spiritual gifts which will help in the decision (1 Cor. 12:8-10, 28- 30; Eph. 4:11; Rom. 12:6-8).

4) Ask yourself the question, "What do I want to do with my life?" The apostle Paul helps us by stating, "Work out your own salvation with fear and trembling; for it is God who works in you both to will and to do for His good pleasure" (Phil. 2:12, 13). The implication is that God is at work encouraging certain feelings within you. The word translated "work" comes from the Greek word *energo*, which is where our word "energy" comes from, He will energize us to find and do His will. This is also taught in the Old Testament: "I will give you a new heart and put a new spirit within you; I will take the heart of stone out of your flesh and give you a heart of flesh. I will put My Spirit

within you and cause you to walk in my statutes, and you will keep my judgments and do them" (Ezek.36:26, 27).

5) Examine the qualifications for the ministry
Try finding in 1Timothy 3:1-7. Notice the word "desires" appears twice in verse one. This indicates a great desire for the ministry. Also note that the qualifications seem to deal more with character than with talent.

6) Realize that some doors may already be closed to you. As a Christian seeking God's will, you can never work in an abortion clinic or be a bartender. Do not seek what is obviously not God's will for you.

7) Take a personal talent inventory to discover your abilities and gifts (Matt. 25:14-30).

8) Begin now to use the talents you have. "You have been faithful over a few things, I will make you

Ruler over many things. Enter into the joy of your lord" (Matt. 25:23). Don't expect God to show you any more than you have already obeyed.

9) List several types of vocations that utilize your talents and skills. There are many vocations open today in Christian ministries: church administration, education, radio and television programming, music, and medical missions are but a few. Do not feel limited to a preaching ministry, but be "soul-conscious" no matter what your occupation is. Be open and ready to share the good news of Christ with others.

10) Talk to those already in the ministries, and ask them to advise you. In I Samuel 3:7-19 we see that Samuel often consulted Eli for advice.

11) Pray and ask the Lord for specific guidance (Prov. 3:5, 6). Begin developing a rich prayer life.

12) Live a holy life. Don't quench and grieve the Holy Spirit of God, for it is He who will guide you into

all truth (John 16:13) and teach you all things (John 14:26). To know the things of God involves being

filled with the Spirit. 13) The key word in the ministry is not ability, but *availability*. The willingness to be a servant and the willingness to sacrifice precede the ability to be a minister literally a "servant").

14) Your present role is important to God. You can only plan tomorrow on what you are willing to do for God today.

15) Seek confirmation of your call from others.

The most important factor to consider in determining God's will is to realize that God calls you, not to a position, but to a Person- to Himself. He calls you to be at His disposal.

- To seek God's will is life's greatest pursuit.

- To know God's will is life's greatest wisdom.

- To do God's will is life's greatest work.

Romans 3:10-18, 23. These verses deal with the fact of man's sin. Romans 6-9. Because of love, Christ died to pay for our sin. Romans 6:23. Sin earns death; eternal life is a gift of God. Romans 10:9. Salvation involves both confession (head knowledge) and faith (commitment of the Heart). Romans 10:13. Our part is to call on Him, to offer Him our lives. Romans 8:1. "There is therefore now no condemnation to those who are in Christ Jesus, who do not walk according to the flesh, but according to the Spirit? We are commanded by Christ to witness: "You shall receive power when the Holy Spirit has come upon you; and you shall be witnesses to Me in Jerusalem, and in all Judea and Samaria, and to the end of the earth" (Acts 1:8). Although it is a command, witnessing should be a spontaneous result of Christ working in our lives. We will have a desire to share the new life we have found. Whether we witness in word or in deed, we should do so with a joyful heart and leave the results to God. "So shall My word be that goes forth from My mouth; it shall not return to Me void, but it shall accomplish what I please, and it shall prosper in the thing for which I sent it" (Is. 55:11). The apostle Paul knew this truth when he wrote, "1 planted, Apollos watered, but God gave the increase" (1Cot. 3:6). There are many written plans available to use in witnessing. However, the most important and forceful tool you will ever use is your own testimony of your personal decision for Christ and what He means to you. Begin by writing a few sentences for each part of the following outline, and then learn to present it smoothly:

1) The need or needs in my life before I was born again (example-loneliness, fear, peer pressure, emptiness).

2) I understood my need for Christ (example-I began to understand sin; a friend shared what Christ had meant to him or her personally).

3) How I was born again (example-I prayed with a friend, I prayed in my room, or I prayed with a counselor during a church service).

4) The differences that occurred in my life when I became a Christian; these should be the opposite of point No. I (example-love instead of loneliness, courage rather than fear, decision to follow Christ instead of the crowd).

5.) I know for sure that I will go to heaven when I die because of God's promises to me.

6) Are any of these things true in your experience?

There are many excellent tracts which can be purchased at your local Christian bookstore. These often have a plan of salvation you can read along with a friend. Also, talk to your pastor or youth leader about enrolling in a witnessing class.

Possibly the most widely used witnessing plan is called "The Roman Road?' It is an easy and effective way to lead someone to a born-again relationship with Christ:

your parents, your teacher, or your employer? That, of course, is deliberate sin against God's chain of authority. Is your pride fueling your temper, when a spirit of humility would help you overcome it? Someone embarrassed you and you want to retaliate. This has the same root as hatred and is sin. Perhaps you will find the need to reevaluate your priorities and eliminate the extra stress tempting you to sin in anger.

But we have the promise of Romans 6:14: "For sin shall not have dominion over you, for you are not under law but under grace?" The first rule to remember in trying to understand your temperament is that not all anger is sinful. Indeed Paul himself instructed us," 'Be angry, and do not sin': do not let the sun go down on your wrath, nor give place to the devil" (Eph. 4:26, 27). It is, therefore, possible to be angry and yet not sin.

Chapter 11

What is Anger?

Anger is a natural response built into every person as a protection from danger. It is a built-in defense system. You may see your parents or other adults experience this as they support and try to lead the family. All of these things we have discussed are situations you must and will continue to face throughout your life.

However, as in every other desire, need, and ability you are endowed with, self-control must be maintained. The more often you allow your anger to get out of control, the more your anger will control *you*. Recognizing your anger problem is your first step toward changing it. The differences that occurred in my life when I became a Christian because I knew where I was going because of God's promises to me. Because of love, Christ died to pay for our sin. Romans 6: 3. Sin earns death; eternal life is a gift of God. Romans 10:9. Salvation involves both confession (head knowledge) and faith (commitment of the heart). Romans 10:13. Our part is to call on Him, to offer Him our lives. (Romans 8:1.) "There is therefore now no condemnation to those who are in Christ Jesus, who do not walk according to the flesh, but according to the Spirit?'

Recognizing your anger problem is your first step toward changing it. Perhaps you will find the need to reevaluate your priorities and eliminate the extra stress tempting you to sin in anger. Anger, therefore, can be described as a response to danger which is apt to be sinful unless we control it. Otherwise anger controls *us*. But we have the promise of Romans 6:14: "For sin shall not have dominion over you, for you are not under law but under grace?" The first rule to remember in trying to understand your temperament is that not all anger is sinful. Indeed Paul himself instructed us," 'Be angry, and do not sin': do not let the sun go down on your wrath, nor give place to the devil" (Eph. 4:26, 27). It is, therefore, possible to be angry and yet not sin. Anger is a natural response built into every person as a protection from danger. It is a built-in defense system. God will go out of His way to show you His will. He wants you to do His will more than you want to do it and so will provide clear guidance. "I will instruct you and teach you in the way you should go" (Ps.32:8).

By God's grace we are enabled to adopt a lifestyle of holiness, that is, obedience to the will of God. With His help, by guarding our minds and emotions, controlling our appetites and desires, we develop holy habits that will remain with us as we grow. So you are able to control your anger and grow in the Lord from day to day.

Many of us too casually inquire about God's will for our lives. If we really want God's best for us, it will become a matter of urgent prayer each day until the answer is clear.

So many times we struggle with decisions already clearly decided and stated by God. The first place to turn in seeking God's will is to the Bible itself. We must first obey what God has already revealed to us concerning His will for our lives. We cannot expect Him to tell us more than we have already obeyed. It is equally important to trust God for your decision, regardless of what the outcome may be. Jesus prayed, "Father, not

My will, but Yours, be done" (Luke 22:42). This can be accomplished only when we realize how very much God loves us and wants the best for our lives. Faith and obedience go together.

If we really want God's best for us, it will become a matter of urgent prayer each day until the answer is clear. Ask yourself, "Just how much time do I spend in prayer asking God to reveal His will?" Instead, it is easier to depend on circumstances as our answer. Yes, God does use circumstances to reveal His will, but circumstances alone are not enough.

Chapter 12

What is the Call to Ministry?

Perhaps it should be pointed out that all people do not find God's will concerning full- time Christian service in the same way. While there is no magic formula, there are biblical principles that should be helpful:

1) God loves you and has a plan for your life. Never forget this truth. He has a unique plan for each day as well as for your Future, You may not know in advance all that this plan involves, but God will

unfold it as you obey and wait on Him.

2) God will go out of His way to show you His will. He wants you to do His will more than you want to do it and so will provide clear guidance. "I

will instruct you and teach you in the way you should go" (Ps. 32:8).

3) God has given you spiritual gifts which will help in the decision (1Cor. 12:8-10, 28- 30; Eph. 4:11; Rom. 12:6-8).

4) Ask yourself the question, "What do I want to do with my life?" The apostle Paul helps us by stating, "Work out your own salvation with fear and trembling; for it is God who works in you both to will and to do for His good pleasure" (Phil. 2:12, 13).

5) Examine the qualifications for the ministry found in 1Timothy 3:1-7. Notice the word "desires" appears twice in verse one. This indicates a great desire for the ministry. Also note that the qualifications seem to deal more with character than with talent.

6) Realize that some doors may already be closed to you. As a Christian seeking God's will, you can

never work in an abortion clinic or be a bartender. Do not seek what is obviously not God's will for you.

7) Take a personal talent inventory to discover your abilities and gifts (Matt. 25:14-30).

8) Begin now to use the talents you have. "You have been faithful over a few things, I will make you

ruler over many things. Enter into the joy of your lord" (Matt. 25:23). Don't expect God to show you any more than you have already obeyed.

10) Talk to those already in the ministries, and ask them to advise you. In I Samuel 3:7-19 we see that Samuel often consulted Eli for advice.

11) Pray and ask the Lord for specific guidance (Prov. 3:5, 6). Begin developing a rich prayer life.

12) Live a holy life. Don't quench and grieve the Holy Spirit of God, for it is He who will guide you into all truth (John 16:13) and teach you all things (John 14:26). To know the things of God involves being filled with the Spirit.

13) The key word in the ministry is not ability, but *AVAILABILITY.* The willingness to be a servant and the willingness to sacrifice precede the ability to be a minister.

14) Your present role is important to God. You can only plan tomorrow on what you are willing to do for God today.

15) Seek confirmation of your call from others.

The most important factor to consider in determining God's will is to realize that God calls you, not to a position, but to a Person- to Himself. He calls you to be at His disposal.• To seek God's will is life's greatest ACCOMPLISHMENT.

Chapter 13

How do I Cope with Death?

Before we can understand death, we must understand life. God's purpose in creating us was not for the life we have now, but so that we might live eternally with Him. These bodies, wonderful as they are, will age, become ill, and wear out. Not so with the new body a Christian receives at the resurrection of all who have died "in Christ?' That body will last forever. There are several questions asked by those who have lost loved ones through death. Fortunately we have a book, the Bible, full of answers for every valid question.

The first question asked is, "What happens to the body at death?" Although you may see a lifeless body lowered into the ground, you need not despair, for the spirit lives on eternally. Instead of remembering a casket or gravesite, think of your loved one's body as a house he or she used to live in. That loved one has moved away, but memories linger on. Jesus has prepared a new house as described in John 14:1, 2-"Let not your heart be troubled; you believe in God, believe also in Me. In My Father's house are many mansions; if it were not so, I would have told you. I go to prepare a place for you?' At Christ's coming the graves will be opened, and the bodies of those who loved Him will be raised up in new life. Another question often asked is, "Will we know each other?" In 1 Corinthians 13:12 the Bible teaches that we will- "For now we see in a mirror, dimly, but then face to face. Now I know in part, but then I shall know just as I also am known?'

Also there is a great desire to be sure the loved one knows of our grief and sorrow, as well as the future we seek to accomplish on earth. Hebrews 12:1 offers this-"Therefore we also, since we are surrounded by so great a cloud of witnesses, let us lay aside every weight, and the sin which so easily ensnares us, and let us run with endurance the race that is set before us?' Not only is our loved one aware of the course of our lives, but we should use this as encouragement to make our lives count to the very fullest as we realize death comes to all of us.

Our happy memories should comfort us, remembering the good times, the love, the sharing. Also the example of the former lives of our loved ones can help us grow stronger. Hope lives on as we remember the final dwelling place for all Christians, where "God will wipe away every tear from their eyes; there shall be no more death, nor sorrow, nor crying; and there shall be no more pain, for the former things have passed away" (Rev. 21:4).

Chapter 14

What is Heaven Like?

Heaven is a prepared place for a prepared people. Jesus told us in John 14:2, "In My Father's house are many mansions; if it were not so, I would have told you. I go to prepare a place for you?' We are told many times of the great multitudes of people in heaven. Jesus gave us the requirement for seeing and entering the kingdom of God, that is, "You must be born again" (John 3:7). We also have scriptural evidence that God the Father (Rev. 4:2, 3), God the Son (Rev. 5:1-7), and God the Holy Spirit (Rev. 14:13) are in heaven, as are also angelic beings (Heb. 12:22; Rev. 5:11). Another group mentioned are twenty-four elders who are seated around the throne of God (Rev. 4:4, 10, 11).

A magnificent description of heaven is detailed in Revelation chapters 21 and 22. Here the holy city is called the New Jerusalem. It will be 1,500 miles square (Rev. 21:16) with a highest point of 1,500 miles, and walls made of jasper measuring 216 feet in height (Rev. 21:17, 18). The foundations of this beautiful city bear the names of the twelve apostles and are decorated with precious stones. Each of the twelve gates (three in each of the four walls) will carry the name of one of the twelve tribes of Israel, and each gate is made of a single pearl (Rev. 21:12, 13, 21). The street of the city is of the purest gold, so that it is clear (Rev. 21:21). Flowing from the throne of God will be a crystal-clear river of the water of life, and on either side will be planted the tree of life, bearing twelve types of fruit every month (Rev. 22:1-3). Even in all of its beauty, heaven is missing some things. It's Missing you and I. How can such glory lack anything? Listen to God's good news: no more hunger, thirst, or excessive heat (Rev. 7:16); no more sea (Rev. 21:1); no more tears (21:4); no more night (21:25); and no more sin (21:27). There shall be no more curse upon the earth because of sin (Rev. 22:3). And last, but not least, Satan will be exiled forever (Rev. 20:10). ARE YOU COMING?? "But there shall by no means enter it anything that defiles, or causes an abomination or a lie, but only those who are written in the Lamb's Book of Life" (Rev. 21:27).

Chapter 15

Is Hell Real?

While the doctrine of eternal punishment is not very popular, it is a major teaching of the Bible. The Greek word *Gehenna,* translated "hell:' appears twelve times in the Greek New Testament. Eleven of those times it is used by Jesus Himself. Jesus, the most compassionate, caring person who ever lived, taught the reality of Hell. Hell is described in detail in Luke 16:19-31. There are those who refer to this passage as a parable rather than a true story. However, Jesus never used proper names in parables as He did in Luke 16, thus proving its accuracy as a true story.

Several facts are known about Hell. Man has a memory in Hell. Abraham asked the rich man to remember his life and the way he had chosen to live. At this suggestion the rich man also remembered his five brothers and begged Abraham to send a warning to them about the torments of Hell (Luke 16:25-28). The unbeliever will remember all the times he might have said "yes" to God but didn't. Man finds no escape from Hades. The rich man begged for water, but Abraham was unable to accommodate him. Abraham spoke of a great gulf that separated them. No one was able to pass between the two places (Luke 16:26).

At the day of judgment, the time comes for us to stand before the Judge-God Himself-and give an account of every deed of our lives, "And they were judged, each one according to his works" (Rev. 20:13). Keep in mind that the unbeliever will be alone. There will be no crowd to blame problems on, no parents to speak in defense. He will not be questioned about the sins of his friends or classmates, nor about the mistakes of his parents. One life and one alone will be on trial-your own, No matter what else has been done, good or bad, the determining factor at that time will be what decision was made about Christ and the gift of eternal life. At that time, the Bible tells us, "And anyone not found written in the Book of Life was cast into the lake of fire" (Rev. 20:15). Hell is not where you want to spend your eternity. As God began to open up his word to me through revelation I was reminded of these scriptures:

- Lake of fire and brimstone (Rev. 20:10, 14, 15);

- Fire that shall never be quenched (Mark 9:43);

- Everlasting fire (Matt. 18:8, g; 25:41);

- Outer darkness (Matt. 8:12; 22:13; 25:30);

- Everlasting punishment (Matt. 2 5:46);

- Weeping and gnashing of teeth (Mali.25:30).

Death brings judgment and hell for the non-Christian. They also serve as a warning to examine ourselves as to whether we truly have been born again, lest we be like the rich man in Luke 16. ITS NOT TOO LATE!!!!

Chapter 16

Will this Guilty Feeling Ever Leave Me?

So Now that you know the Truth will this guilty feeling leave me. A guilty conscience about sin is a sign that the Holy Spirit of God is showing us impurity in our lives. This is called "conviction" and is the first step in obtaining forgiveness of sin. We must have true sorrow and then a change of heart toward the sin, causing us to forsake it completely. This is called "repentance;' "turning around," or "changing our minds" about sin.

When we give our lives to Christ and receive Him as Savior, He forgives every sin in our past completely. And the forgiveness of God is even more wonderful than this, for He tells us, "I, even

I, am He who blots out your transgressions for My own sake, and I will not remember your sins" (Is. 43:25). He not only forgives, He forgets! We cannot judge God's forgiveness by man's ability to forgive.

Once we have confessed our sins, we must move forward to the future of living for God. "If we confess our sins, He is faithful and just to forgive us..." (1John 1:9). The word "confess" literally means "to agree with?' God hates sin; so must we must turn from it. "Therefore, if anyone is in Christ, he is a new creation; old things have passed away; behold, all things have become new" (2 Cor. 5:17). Yes, you can become pure in God's eyes. So then, a guilty conscience comes with the act of sin, but should not continue after confession. "'Come now, and let us reason together,' says the Lord, 'though your sins are like scarlet, they shall be as white as snow; though they are red like crimson, they shall be as wool'" (Isa. 1:18).

If you are having a problem forgiving yourself and others; read God's verses on forgiving and forgetting over and over, and believe them. Then claim Philippians 3:13, 14-"Brethren, I do not count myself to have apprehended [reached the goal]; but one thing I do, forgetting those things which are behind and reaching forward to those things which are ahead, I press toward the goal for the prize of the upward call of God in Christ Jesus?"

Chapter 17

Will God Stop Loving Me?

A common fear is that we might commit a sin so great or so often that it would cause God to turn His love away from us. This is because we cannot understand the eternal love with which God loves us. His love cannot be compared to human love, for man's love often changes with circumstances. Not so with God's love. The Bible tells us, "For God so loved the world...?' And He gives eternal life to those in the world who genuinely trust Him"...that whoever believes in Him should...have everlasting life" (John 3:16). And that wonderful love never ends. "For I am persuaded that neither death nor life, nor angels nor principalities nor powers, nor things present nor things to come, nor height nor depth, nor any other created thing, shall be able to separate us from the love of God which is in Christ Jesus our Lord" (Rom. 8:38, 39). In short, nothing can change God's love toward us. God's love is eternal and arises out of His decision to love us; that is, it is not merited by our actions. We must learn to enjoy this truth, but be careful not to abuse it. To have the attitude of living as we wish, without giving thought to God's will, is foolish. "What shall we say then? Shall we continue in sin that grace may abound? Certainly not! How shall we who died to sin live any longer in it?" (Rom. 6:1).

God is not to be taken for granted. We are told, "Do not be deceived, God is not mocked; for whatever a man sows, that he will also reap" (Gal. 6:7). Our lives should be lived out of gratitude and adoration for a God who loves us, blesses us, and cares for every part of our lives. Jesus Himself taught in the temple in Jerusalem, "My sheep hear My voice, and I know them, and they follow *Me*. And I give them eternal life, and they shall never perish; neither shall anyone snatch them out of My hand. My Father, who has given them to Me, is greater than all; and no one is able to snatch them out of My Father's hand. I and My Father are one" (John 10:27-30).

Chapter 18

What is Unforgivable Sin?

This subject has caused understandable concern among many people. The phrase "unpardonable sin" is not found in the Bible, but it is the usual way of referring to the blasphemy against the Holy Spirit (Matt. 12:31, 32; Mark 3:28, 29; Luke 12:10). Blasphemy is defiant hostility toward God. There is much difference of opinion about the meaning of blasphemy against the Holy Spirit, but it refers primarily to the sin of decisively and finally rejecting the testimony of the Holy Spirit regarding the person and work of Jesus Christ. It is the ultimate rejection of the Son of God, just as the Pharisees are described as doing in this passage. Jesus' miracles authenticated His person and mission as the Son of God. Rather than admitting his divine power, the Pharisees reject it and claimed His power came from Satan. Anyone who witnesses evidence of the Lord's power, and finally declares it to be satanic, exhibits a condition of the heart beyond divine illumination and therefore hopeless. Jesus affirms that all the sins of people can be forgiven, with this one fearful exception. Blasphemy against the Holy Spirit forever removes a person beyond the place where forgiveness is possible. If a young person rejects Christ and His salvation and dies in that condition, he or she will perish eternally.

In Mark 3:30 we are told that they accused Jesus of being inhabited by a demon. Such blasphemy reveals a sinful heart. Our speech usually is the expression of what is in our hearts

Are you worrying about having committed the unpardonable sin? If so, consider closely what the Bible teaches, not what others say. The unpardonable sin is final rejection of the truth concerning Jesus Christ. He alone can save us from our sins. Have you rejected Christ in your own life? Then you must, without delay accept the truth about Christ, humble yourself, turn from your sin, and personally receive Christ as your Lord and Savior. Do not risk the real possibility of irreversibly and finally hardening yourself against the witness of the Spirit regarding Jesus Christ. Do not go out into eternity without hope, without Jesus.

CHAPTER 19

How Can I Stop Following the Crowd?

Following the crowd has led many people into a life contrary to all they have ever been taught and believed. This has been my testimony since the age of 16 years old. It occurs because one of our greatest needs is to be accepted by others. Overcoming this trap can be accomplished as a Christian.

First, realize that your own strength is not enough. Jesus was tempted as 'we are, yet He did not sin. How could this be possible? The answer is found in the book of Matthew where Jesus was tempted by Satan himself. Jesus said three times, "It is written" (Matt. 4:4, 7, 10). He was referring to the Word of God. Just as Christ found strength to overcome temptation through the Word of God, so can we. Another very important factor in overcoming pressure from your peer group is previous decision making. There are many pitfalls you can avoid by predetermining your answer or action to a tempting situation. For example, if you have already studied the Bible teaching on sex, and vowed to God to keep sexually pure, you won't have to wonder what to do if you are asked to engage in sex. If you make up your mind before the fact, the temptation will not be so great. You will much more likely give into the crowd if your decisions haven't been made before hand. Choosing your friends carefully is essential to staying on the right track in life. Get involved with Christian friends. You can meet them through your church groups, Sunday school and Bible clubs. Make sure you are in full attendance with your church on a weekly basis. You need spiritual food for strength, which is only available to the saints of God.

Chapter 20

Is it Possible to Control My Thoughts

and Desires?

It has often been said, "I can't stop a bird from landing on my head, but I can sure keep him from building a nest there!" Temptations come to us. We have decisions to make in life. We are affected by the things we see and hear. By grace we are given the power to choose those things which will occupy our minds and determine our morality. We can end the tempting desire or thought before it becomes sin. We have the example of Jesus to encourage us: "For we do not have a High Priest who cannot sympathize with our weaknesses, but was in all points tempted as we are, yet without sin" (Corinth. 4:15). It is important to learn to control ourselves. An uncontrolled person may bring great harm to himself and others. Sexual thoughts and desires are no different from other thoughts in terms of needing control. Our spending habits must be controlled, or we will be financially bankrupt. Our thoughts must be controlled, or we may become emotionally unbalanced. Our actions must be controlled to avoid spiritual suicide. The need for control of sexual thoughts and desires does not end at marriage, because many circumstances, such as pregnancy, illness, children, traveling, and work schedules, will make it necessary. Possibly the best way to overcome wrong thoughts and desires is to avoid temptation as much as possible. That is, stay away from those acquaintances who encourage you wrongly; don't be alone with anyone you are sexually attracted to, "Flee also youthful lusts; but pursue righteousness, faith, love, peace with those who call on the Lord out of a pure heart" (2 Tim. 2:22). God offers help for coping with both the desires of the body and the thoughts of the mind, which really are the same. In Romans 12:1, 2 we are told to "present (our] bodies a living sacrifice, holy, acceptable to God, which is [our] reasonable service. And do not be conformed to this world, but be transformed by the renewing of [our] mind, that [we] may prove what is that good and acceptable and perfect will of God." If we earnestly and completely commit our bodies to God, we will not be so quick to offer ourselves to another outside of marriage. The Christian actually has no right to defile his or her body: "Do you not know that your body is the temple of the Holy Spirit who is in you, whom you have from God, and you are not your own? For you were bought at a price therefore glorify God in your body and in your spirit, which are God's" (1 Cor. 6:19, 20). "But," you say, "I can't keep the thoughts out of my mind?' But remember what we said in the beginning: "We can end the desire or thought before it becomes sin?' Also, God offers practical help in His Word. "The peace of God, which surpasses all understanding, will guard your hearts and minds through Christ Jesus" (Phil. 4:7). The peace of God is found in spiritual growth, in prayer, and in faith trusting God with every area of life. We must learn to stand on His promise. Finally, to eliminate evil thoughts and desires is not enough. Evil thoughts must be replaced by good thoughts.

Chapter 21

IS Sex Wrong If you are Really In Love?

Many psychologists believe that the average teenage female falls in and out of love at least ten times. The teenage male falls in and out of love about half as many times. Obviously, if you give yourself sexually to everyone you feel affection for you will be sexually and emotionally scarred, as well as spiritually bankrupted. As a result, the possibility of a fulfilling relationship with the mate God has chosen for you

Become decisions. Learn that man was not created for himself, nor was he created for sex, In spite of the sexual obsession popularized by society. Genesis 1:26-28 tells us we were created by God, for God, and in the likeness of God. This means we will not be fulfilled or satisfied, never be complete, without Him. The Bible tells us that He gave every one of the animals a mate. Genesis 2:18 also says that it is not good for man to be alone. However, sex is held in high esteem throughout the pages of the Bible, and is considered holy. It is not cheap or dirty when practiced in accordance with God's design. It is the consummation of marital love, a satisfying joy, a special task, and a sacred trust. There are some who claim the Bible teaches sex only as a means to replenish the earth. Certainly procreation is the primary reason for sex. However, if that had been God's full intention, He could just as easily have had us plant a lock of hair or a toenail clipping, wait nine months, and "harvest" a child. God's idea of sex is a gift enjoyed by a husband and wife resulting in completeness, close communion, and a special bonding. This is why the Bible speaks of sexual union as "knowing" one's mate.

Several sexual sins are mentioned in the Bible. Fornication is the sexual act committed by those who are not married. When a married man or woman commits the sexual act with someone other than his marriage mate, both sexual partners are committing the sin of adultery. The unnatural act of sex between two women or two men is called homosexuality. God describes this as vile affection and shameful. (See the answer to question 36, "Is Homosexuality a Sin?" for more information.) There are seven lists of evil in the New Testament Fornication heads the list six times and is mentioned second in the seventh list. Read 1 Corinthians 6:9-20 for a clear and helpful section of Scripture. Verses 13-20 in particular teach that sexual immorality is a sin against the body and injures the soul. The ultimate reason to abstain from sex before marriage is because premarital sex is sin against God. But there are other problems to consider in this behavior. First, there is the very real risk of pregnancy. The incidence of pregnancy among the young is alarmingly high. Do not think it cannot happen to you. It can, on the first time, on the fifth time, anytime. It is possible. A second problem of the sin of fornication is the cheapening of your testimony. Yes, there will be talk about your actions. Is this the way you want to represent Christ in your life?

Also you have opened yourself to the ease of falling into this sin again and again, Saying "No" the first time is difficult, but once you have ignored your conscience, it will be increasingly easier to continue. You are introducing yourself to a lifestyle that you were never meant to experience as a Christian. You have begun a life of rebellion against God. Finally, as soon as you enter the sexual relationship, you begin to weaken the strengthening of the other areas of your relationship. Knowing each other involves so much. What are the goals in your lives? What habits do you have that might be annoying to the other? Are the ideals and ethics of your lives the same? Do you have the same thoughts on raising children? There are so many avenues to explore in the dating relationship as you prepare for marriage. Many divorces are the result of incompatibility-aspects about each other learned after marriage that were not explored in dating, because the two were drawn together and held by a sexual relationship. A relationship cemented by sex offers a counterfeit completeness, a false closeness, which is often mistaken for love.

Chapter 22

What Area of My Life Am I holding back from God?

Life can be very difficult if you try to live it with your own will and power. While Growing up I had to truly decide that everything that had hurt me and prevented me from living a God fearing life was by the choices and decisions that I had made. It was because I hadn't completely surrendered to God. It was because I had put conditions on how far I was going to allow God in. Before your life can change you must be willing to give yourself away. This means that you must allow yourself to be fully in. I often asked the question "Are you Out are or You In" This is such an important question because if not you will live your life in emotions and feeling and not truly seek the path that God has for your life. Whether it's Pride or Fear Complete surrender and recognizing that you can't hold anything back from God must be your final decision. Come on He knows everything anyway. He is just waiting for you to come and reason with him. Isaiah 1:18 Come now, and let us reason together, saith the Lord: though your sins be as scarlet, they shall be as white as snow: though they be red like crimson, they shall be as wool.

AUTHORS WORK

Many Questions: What Area of My Life am I holding back from God?

Get Fit With Jesus Christ In 90 days?

How to Unlock the Chamber to A Repentant Heart?

CONTACT THE AUTHOR@mwfi.weebly.com

Made in the USA
Middletown, DE
03 September 2024

60287719R00070